Ink and Afterlight

Tarini Jamwal

For nani (grandma),

Whenever people tell me I have every bit of your talent, nothing makes me prouder

Acknowledgments

I would like to express my heartfelt thanks to all my friends and family who've always encouraged me to pursue my passion for writing. You've helped me live my dreams. To everyone who has ever inspired me, or shared in my excitement —thank you. And to all those who have paused to read this book, I hope the words in these verses find you when you need them the most and settle in your heart. I'm truly grateful for your support.

"You can justify anything, if you do it poetically enough"

...

Contents

CONTENTS

CONTENTS

1. Unit 1*:* Spring

Spring: 'passion'

2. The Poet

The clock ticks midnight

The poet pores over the pages

When the sky goes black and the moon howls

The miracle starts for ages

The poet

He finds beauty even in a dying bush of rose

Tangled thoughts, simple prose

"Oh your poems are truly beautiful!"

"Your mind must be a field of daffodils"

Little do they know, the poet's mind's a brewing storm

One's most inexpressible feelings does he adorn

The poet

Bleeds his emotions onto paper

Never to disappoint, a timeless creature

He either doesn't write for weeks or writes for hours on end

There's no in- between, no way to pretend

The dark academia, the steaming tea

The poet finds beauty even in misery

His trust in the written word,

Holding conviction it can change the world

The greatest fortune, none can deny

Is to live in a poet's eye

His verse ensures you never die

His mind, a trapdoor

Once you enter it, there's no exit for sure

The poet

Exemplary of a wizard

His art, an occult, whisks together magic

Speaks one's mind in ballads utterly tragic

The poet

Always writing, never the one being written about

Write him a love note and he'll treasure it throughout

Even in moments of utmost solitude

The poetic mind doesn't know quietude

Laughing quietly, his mind astray

Wondering if he'll ever be good enough someday

3. Passion

Once you find out what you love

Let it consume you every day

For the most sacred path to happiness

Is to follow its way

Let passion set you ablaze

With a flame so bright, illuminating your darkest days

An investment that makes you lose track of time

Passion is an energy so sublime

There are things you would die for

And ones you would kill for

But the most precious ones are what you live for

That's passion, let it set you ablaze

And help you journey with fulfilment through life's maze

4. The Moon

A crescent silver scar

In midnight's dark skin

Offers a silent hearing

To all of my whims

The moon is my best count on

Even when the darkness is gone

It pulls the oceans and my heart alike

But the plot twist goes like

It whispers its secrets too

Like how it has a borrowed glow

But no one really knows

5. 3 A.M.

The Devil's Hour is really for the restless souls

Why does everything make sense at 3:00 a.m.?

The writer's block seems to be cured

In the dead of the night's cold

The overthinkers' slumber

Suddenly becomes non-existent

Like being drunk all this while, then suddenly becoming sober

That time of the night belongs to

The dreamers who can't sleep

The one- sided lovers in pain

Knowing all their efforts will be in vain

"Why does everything make sense at 3:00 a.m.?"

Think the ones broken like glass shards

Hopeless, spending the night counting the stars

The witching hour is for those believers

Who consume themselves today

Knowing they'd enjoy a satisfactory sleep one day

When they've shown their best at play

Why does everything make sense at 3:00 a.m.?

As if the universe has presented a magical number

The world around you is consumed in slumber

Not a soul on the street

Only the mind dares to wander

6. Midnight Bells Resound

In the hush of midnight's silent sway

Where time's tender threads softly fray

A notebook untouched, blank, pristine

Akin to a story yet to be written, unveils a year yet to be seen

A calendar unfolds its wings

As the new year, in splendor, springs

The magic of new beginnings; brought forth

A rebirth of dreams, and their infinite worth

O great mentor, you shower us with light

In wisdom's glow, you shine so bright

As the clock strikes 12, its chime resounds

A symphony of hopes, new bounds

Through seasons of growth, like nature's rhyme

You've enlightened young minds all the time

May your teachings ripple through the years

Alleviating young minds of all their fears

10

As the midnight bells echo and chime

Awaits an epic to behold in the chronicles of time

In the tapestry of time's design

With gratitude, our hearts entwine

...

7. Ascend

You know you're doing good

When the goal excites you

And from where you once stood,

You feel the distance, a gap you've bridged

That's testimony enough of what you've accomplished

A little faith is most of what it takes

Fear shatters, and the comfort zone breaks

Although, there is a catch —

This isn't the final match

You didn't come this far only to halt at the threshold

There's a long road ahead, destiny still has lots to behold

So dear believer — it's showtime, finally

The clock has ticked ruthlessly

It's time to shed your shadows

And put yourself out there, rising unto your greatest glow

8. Unit 2: Summer

Summer: 'love'

9. Hourglass

I laid barefoot on the grass

In the fleeting kiss of the moon's silver light

A wavering apparition, illuminated by the stars —

My dear wallflower, brought to the limelight

Where have you been, all these years?

Not a witness to my cries and tears

Every night, amidst the murmurs of a world half- asleep

By the river my heart weeps

There stands the hourglass, its sands running thin

Slowly counting the days since we let silence win

But the glass reflects your face, soft and bright

Cooler than the breeze, brighter than the starlight

10. Whirlwind Romance

She was the rain

He was the sea

Their love flowed endlessly

Her falling tears, his rising tide

Ever adding to each other's lives

Each drop she gave, the sea would keep

A fulfilled promise, so pure and deep

11. Black Rose

He's like cigarettes and roses

But he's apples and oranges

He's both salt and sugar

He's solitude and anger

He bites his lip, he tosses his hair

I smile like crazy when he says he doesn't care

Affectionate glistening almond eyes

That familiar scent gives me butterflies

His eyes crinkle as a smile flashes across his lips

A mesmerizing aura, gives my heart the skips

12. Sinking Into Oblivion

Sleep's comforting blanket devours me

As I drift off into silence, peace and reverie

Adversity dissolves as I inch closer to my slumber

Like water sizzling on a burnt-out ember

The brush of pillows, cool and deep

Cradles me in the hands of sleep

The moon's mint coolness shines through the pane

A subtle hint of silver, lit by the whistling wane

My feet are safely tucked away in the creases of the quilt;

Just like the worries my mind now lacks

The soft velvet pools around my back

As I sink into an unending seabed of deep sleep

How convenient an escape to evade life

Akin to a parallel life sans worries and strife

Medusa's curse: I'm a rock

Turns into a blessing when I sleep like one

Only stolen when I'm falling in love or falling apart

Sleep: I cherish you and love you with all my heart

Sometimes the best part of my day

When nothing seems to go my way

13. Blue

O nly if you knew, how much I love you

B y thinking about the girl you love, life drowns me in blue

S omething about this love makes me so crazily obsessed

E very encounter leaves my mind foggy and hazy

S low, the obsession is slow, but quick to make me depressed

S till, I know all I can offer you is silent, wistful stares

I t forces me to call you every night in my prayers

O bsessive, unhealthy, futile, and just not good for me

N evertheless, sheds my tears and crushes my hopes infinitely

14. Teenage Love

Strong like the wind, like violent waves of the ocean crashing

Like an overload of emotions roller-coastering, but somehow slow

Her heart crawled up and down her chest, oh, he was dashing

Deep- set eyes, a calming voice, and a pretty smile aglow

In his charcoal eyes, she was a spirit so wholesome

Sea-green eyes and golden skin, reminded him of the ocean

Akin to the perpetually pretty petals of a blooming primrose

She was a song stuck in his mind, his senses afroze

Sharing of stolen glances during Algebra

Sliding chocolate bars in each other's lockers discreetly

Scribbling up anonymous love notes, a sweet enigma

Hiding their feelings, yet yearning for each other completely

15. Honeydew

If every happy memory with you was a precious stone, diamond or gold

I'd have the most beautiful necklace in the world

If every flower symbolized your resilience and strength

I'd be watering the prettiest garden on earth

If every snowflake glistening in the dawn signified your affectionate glow

Nothing would better melt and sizzle my acid tears than the numbing snow

If the copious stars in the sky symbolized every second of time you've sacrificed for me

I'd be looking at the most endless Milky Way there would be

If every color signified the qualities of a perfect mother

I'd be looking at the most colorful painting ever

16. Unbroken

Our friendship's like music, it never gets old

It's worth more than rubies, diamonds, or gold

So I met this girl, our hearts melted and fused,

"Oh she's so much like me!" I thought,

understanding ebbed and oozed

As time flew by, we got closer and closer

She held me together when I thought my world was getting over

She told me it was fine to cut off fake friends

We talked about love, friendship, and the latest trends

Soon, she became one of the greatest pillars of support for me

And I realized my world was right beside me

As we share thoughts, passions, and dreams anew

Our bond glistens, steadfast and true

17. Chasm

Don't leave my heart all right, at least leave my mind

So I can be at peace

And stop counting the days until you're mine

Your eyes once windows, are now mere walls

They don't even meet mine

I'm standing on the edge, about to face a pitfall

I can no longer find stillness in silence

As if I were on the end of a burning cliff

Like vapors of the burning fire, my heart feels adrift

18. Ink And Blood

My cat put on a spectacle last night

A four- legged furball in the candlelight

A confident leap, careless and bold

Knocked over my blue inkwell, spilling a story untold

Glass met the floor, a sudden break

Shards all over, like stars reflected in a midnight lake

Then came the crimson, a deeper stain

The poor creature shivered in pain

What do I love more?

The ink is it, or the blood?

Of- course the blood

My adorable fuzzball, soft and small

Ink can be spilled, but you, not at all

19. Bittersweet

He hadn't read a more beautiful poem

Than the words she planted on his lips

This one was deep, wine- red

Stole his breath, gave his heart the skips

This one was dark chocolate

Bittersweet on his lips

20. Aphrodite

Beauty embodied and pushed out into the world

A heavenly form that walks this earth

She's the queen of the queens

Her presence intoxicating

As the candles light up, celebrating

Ivory skin and long lustrous tresses

Woven into beautiful amber- colored coils

Golden dress plates, gold trinkets

Embellish her rippling satin attire

Her aura is chilling hellfire

Flower laurels crown her brow

An ever- shifting eye color, gorgeous every time

With the ability to replicate the face of the beholder's desire

She moulds each dream, a vision to inspire

Doves trail her, just like whispered lore

Souls kiss the earth she sets foot on, desiring more

Golden roses, and red anemones bloom off her feet

A Greek goddess of grace so sweet

A heavenly scent locked into her

Just like the gaze of her fortunate beholder

21. Unit 3: Monsoon

Monsoon: 'hope'

22. Faith

'He' is the liberating truth of life

Solace in the darkness, mediation in strife

In a world of betrayal, ambush, trust breaks

Hear his voice reverberate in thy heartaches

Smile through tears of disappointment

Accept the storm, insufferable and poignant

For soon thy pain will turn everything around

And develop into happiness, pure and profound

23. Teenage Turmoil

//13//

Mirror, mirror on the wall

I'm so sick of being the ugliest of all

"Just be the angel you are," says Mother

But how do I make friends with her?

//14//

She always thought he was her sun and stars

Only to realize his love only ever left scars

Sick of ex-girlfriends, miniskirts and hair extensions

Fake, gossip girls begging for attention

//15//

He always tried hard to fit in

And gave it his everything

But despite his efforts to make friends

He ended up all alone in the end

//16//

Hiding feelings, heads in the clouds

Trying to shut away from the crowds

"If only someone would understand!"

All this turmoil we can no longer stand

All we need in life's wild ride

A shoulder to lean on through every stride

In others opinions our strength may wane

Yet true power lies in self-reign

Maybe we realize we all feel the same way

And not pretend to be something else, someday

We're all lonely, anxious, full of self-doubt

But together with honesty, there's a way out

24. Playlist

People are like playlists

If every song was a different mood

They hit the shuffle on their own

What's in store for today, that's unknown

Each one flows in its own prelude

People are like playlists

Influenced and inspired by ideas, they're made

A beautiful symphony of good and bad

When listening to their songs being played

You can feel angry, passionate, inspired or sad

You wish to hear some again and again

Some make you feel nostalgic and you delve into déjà vu

A feeling felt before, and you're down memory lane

People are like playlists

Some hit different, what you never saw coming

One can instantly become your favourite, so stunning

Some are ones you could go on playing forever and ever

They never get old, change you for the better

Some are ones that make you heal

And after listening to which, with problems you can deal

Like the songs they hold, they come in different shades

And if it's not the one for you, there are endless upgrades

25. Crimson Optimism

She's not afraid to set foot on the bloody battlefield

Never intimidated by the Grim Reaper, her discomforts concealed

Trudging onto lands whether close or far

Indefinitely standing tall, appearing at the stars

She's a willow, eternally withstanding the wind

Resilience and effervescence whisper from within

Courage is her ride or die

Fresh like the golden sunrise painting the sky

She'll be the driver in command

When her truckload of dreams settles into gears

Akin to the fire in her veins, her sacrifices are crimson

'She' is a woman, a woman with vision

26. Essence

The question will always be

What is *real* beauty?

It doesn't matter if you've an acne-infested face

It's not hot red pimples that make you ugly, but a heart full of hate

Her hair may be more "beautiful" than mine

But as long as I make my heart prettier, I know I'll be fine

Her body may be lither and leaner than mine,

But the beauty of the soul matters more than a sharp jawline

Her platinum- brown bangs may be gorgeous

But a pure and kind heart is way more precious

Her perfect pearly white smile may be "nicer" and

more charming than mine,

But what's more attractive is a spirit that makes

one so fine

Her petite and "perfect" figure may display a

smaller numeral on the scale,

But no amount of glowing skin can hide a personality that's stale

Her chiseled features, lithe brows, and magnetic eyes

may be show-stopping

But a serene, passionate soul is far more jaw- dropping

Her killer fashion sense may be the "hottest" in

town,

But what if I don't need to be society's "10/10",

don't need to look like "her" to be a queen with her crown?

27. Dawnrise

The cuddly *meower*, in a watchful sprawl

Was curled up by her feet

Enjoying the rain's soft script against the wall

The sky shifted colors to light from dark

Just like her future, lit by a little spark

She poured over the pages, her mind a quiet storm

Her faith in the power of ink and thought

Glistening, like the fulfilment her heart sought

28. Stigma

Why is it always "commerce or science?"

Why is it always NEET or JEE

A rigid path they force us to see

The stigma stings just a little too much

The condemnation by society, it's heavy and loud

Crushing dreams beneath its crowd

"Never humanities", they say

"It's a baseless future anyway"

Why create a false rippling illusion

That leads millions to a stereotypical conclusion

Success is not always a white coat or a coding screen

Then why use it to define one's worth, their calibre unseen?

Why make it seem like a non-existent choice

Like a dumpster of "weak" brains

Why instill it into society and children's minds

Why is it always "commerce or science?"

When will it be "humanities, commerce, or science?"

Why not let each path go undeviated, adding its own value to society

And break through this cage, refusing to be prisoners of social piety

29. Ebony

The thirsty crow

Flew and sat on the tree

Caked in snow, the branch gleamed ivory

The crow glared in the pot's water, clear and still

Tipped its beak, a silent spill

Gave my thirst an aching fill

The thirsty crow didn't use pebbles this time

And flew off into the distance, dropping a shimmering dime

30. Monsoon Musings

God put shackles on the scorching heat

As the monsoon had begun

The breeze twisted and turned above the street

As the cuckoos and Koels sung

We were brimming with elation

What a wonderful sensation

Pleasant petrichor everywhere

That monsoon aura lingered in the air

The disappointment of the last period starting in school

Longing to stay for a bit more, to enjoy the weather so cool

The news of a free period in the ground, made us let out joyous shouts

Our spirits soared, as cheers and laughter echoed all about

Our felicity was something we certainly couldn't contain

Instinctively, we put ourselves out there in the rain

Splashed around, jumped in puddles, and danced the period
away

Instead of a humdrum regular day, it became the best-ever
Monday

31. Unit 4*:* Autumn

Autumn: 'feelings'

32. Autumn

The leaves rust red and crispen, embellishing the trees

Amber- maroon as far as the eye can see

Fall, fall, fall, everywhere

In the rustling hymn of crimson, how can one despair?

A red carpet, sprawled underneath

I can catwalk, rejuvenating every time I breathe

There's something about that autumn-infused aura

The cider's sweet fragrance aligns with that of the rusted flora

I could sit for hours on end, wonder-gazed

As if all my problems were somehow erased

Or perhaps I wish to snooze under the bare trees

Hibernating while not having a single care

Only to wake up when the ground is snow- laden and fair

33. *What If*

What if echoes didn't just repeat sound

Instead, whispered secrets from a parallel universe

What if what goes around doesn't come around

Only to be doubled and given to the next person

What if the poet was just a wizard, conjuring occult

What if this life were one big daydream and delusion

What if the reflection we saw before us was the real entity

And we were the illusion?

What if our dreams each night were just glimpses of the parallel
life

That we live at night, to flee from strife

What if we got another chance at our childhood

And are unable to grow up, till we gear up good

What if déjà vu was just our soul trying to revisit our past life

What if everyone under this sun was friends, and we had no foes

What if shadows carried secrets, deep and sweet

How heavy would yours be?

Just how vast can this life be

If human experiences were deeper

How would we play this game called "life"

If the path of untamed human imagination was brought to life?

34. *Hometown Lure*

Endowed with ethereal scenic beauty

From valleys to mountains and cascading falls

Bestowed with picturesque views and tranquility

A deep sense of peace within me calls

Sun-kissed waters, rich forests, and an exhilarating view

The sky gleams in colourful hues, the mist feels new

The crickets' calming chirps adorn the salty breeze

With jasmines' sweet trace, a euphoria that frees

Adventure flows, with no end in sight

Through sacred caves and hills bathed in golden light

Nature draws you in and draws you out

O! What a blissful journey is this throughout

35. Iron And Quartz

Two hands trapped in glass

Bound by quartz, steel, or brass

With hands that spin, it claims our sight

Funny, isn't it?

We let it rule our day

This little trick- we follow its way

Chasing the ticking, we blindly pursue

Letting that solder of steel and tin tell us what to do

The illusion of "time" it holds

Is enough to speed up our heart's pace

When against time, we're in a race

36. *Untamed Thoughts*

Reclined by the serene poolside

Not brushing my thoughts aside

Nothing to do

Reflecting on life, a date with the real me- so overdue

I do not fret; funky jazz echoes as cold waves crash ashore

The icy blue, cotton candy studded heaven overhead, so azure

Happiness so pure after many, many years

Clear as the water, washing away my tears

A peaceful, exhilarating bliss was so long ago

The sun soaks my skin as the minty breeze twists and blows

Chlorine lightly whisks in my nose, an earthly place yet so
paradisaical

A dream oh-so fantastical

The sun-kissed waters rejuvenate my mind and purify my soul

An unproductive yet soul-shaping hour, leaves me feeling so
whole

37. *Clashing Personalities*

Thousands of feelings trapped within me

Some happy buzzing inside, some struggling to be set free

Sometimes, my subconscious clouds itself with anxiety

While oft-times, the cockles of my heart dance with gaiety

As I open my wings and gear up to fly

Admiring the wishing star scud past the sky

Apprehensions make me doubtful and insecure

Yet my heart emboldens me to fearlessly explore

Weird innerscapes and clashing personalities

Yet what holds my individuality

Although there's always a yin to a yang

There's a part of life many oft leave blank

Joy, spunk, delight, exhilaration

Priceless emotions beyond expression

Life- a blissful journey filled with rejuvenation

Ignites within me cheer, passion, and anticipation

Realizing this world is a realm of unlimited possibility

My pensive mind oft becomes a paragon of positivity

Those feelings on top of the world and over the moon

Spur my heart to exhibit more and more gratitude

38. Unit 5*:* Winter

Winter: 'melancholy'

39. Nostalgia

Remember life when...

Making friends was as easy as a game of rock, paper, scissors

Summer breaks were days of freedom then

Golden days, untouched by life's blizzards

Saturday princess movies were my reason for living

Amidst those charms, I couldn't be more oblivious to overthinking

Those fancy fashion shows with Mom as the judge

When between my sister and I there was no such thing as a "grudge"

Being a model, astronaut and pilot was my childhood dream

Now it's hard to pass math without letting out a few screams

Wonder what happened to those precious golden hours,

When competition meant who could pluck more flowers?

When cousins' meet-ups were the coolest days

When nothing could compare to the joy of my birthday

When I wished to be taken to Narnia or Camp Half-Blood

Now, I stress over "AIIMS or Harvard?"

Wish I could rewind time and freeze it

Another day of tumbling in the grass

While wishing upon the twinkling stars

Totally unaware of the passing- by hours

40. Forlorn

The idea of love seems extinct sometimes

It seems a surreal relic that travelled through time

Only seems apparent in ephemeral fairy tales

Like burning embers on the brink of ash, the warmth pales

It's hard to believe you are wanted, valid, and accepted

When clouded with deceptive illusions, feeling dejected

Marred by flaws and faults, cast aside like a shattered spear

When all you want to do is retreat, recoil, and disappear

When you feel misunderstood, judged, and condemned

There's a rocky, dark road ahead with no way to mend

Left all alone to cry and fall

How do you rise above it all?

That's left to you, dear friend

41. Snowflake

I sat lost, chin in hands, as the cold window wept

Each "tear" a mirror of snow that'd slept

The window cracked; a breeze pushed through

A single snowflake crossed into view

It spiraled down, a fleeting guest

In the amber hues of my freshly brewed coffee

It came to a rest

I glared beyond the frost-kissed glass

Where time dissolved in moments that passed

42. Goodbyes

From your heart I was easily replaced

From your mind I was easily erased

My mind's grown restless, restless of the "we're great

 friends" charade I've been putting on

I've been so awfully used, but I still hate to think you're gone

Didn't you say a million times you'd be there for me?

Yet here we are, your disloyalty's on fire

Suddenly you're gone, you manipulative liar

I always thought, your sugar-coated words wounded

up to sound tearfully beautiful

But believing them was the bane of my existence, all of

them ever so painful

Still, you'll never know just how much I love you

Just how thinking about the broken parts of our

friendship takes me in the blues

43. *Wound*

Can you fix some relationships, even when love turns to hate?

Or is losing some important people just fate?

Somewhere between hello and goodbye there was love

Somewhere between where you wouldn't love me enough

44. Wraith

It lurks in the shadows

I bat an eyelid, it vanishes

A hushed manoeuvre

But it never perishes

Amidst the merciless dark

It blends seamlessly

Only revealing occasionally-

A pair of blazing eyes

Displaying menacing avarice

45. Granules

An anxiety-ridden being

I falter

Everything slowly muffles and amplifies

As the void opens up wide

Sweat, but cold, clings

Tremors slow my step

Each motion is heavy and hollow

Skin crispens, becomes more olive

Folding into itself

I shake and tremble

I crumble

Unto dust I return

46. Recurring

I'm standing on the same path I fled from

Perhaps I was destined to complete a full circle

And gyrate in the storm

Realizing only when I retrospect, all this seems comical

All the better, I should propel forward

For time is not a line etched in the sand

But is a wheel, presenting itself again and again

And any amount of regret will forever go in vain

61

The end,

Where time, memory and your feelings gently blend.